RESCUING JFK

How Solomon Islanders Rescued John F. Kennedy and the Crew of PT-109

Written by:
Alan Elliott and Annie Kwai
Illustrated by: Evelyn Morgan

Rescuing JFK: How Solomon Islanders Rescued John F. Kennedy and the Crew of the PT-109

Dedication: To the brave Coastwatchers and Scouts [MM1] who served during World War II in the Solomon Islands.

Acknowledgments: Many thanks to those who helped with this project. These include Sir Bruce Saunders KBE, OBE, Dennis McAdams, Wilson Gina, and Patricia Summey. Additional thanks to Cindy Rodella-Purdy for her talents and skills in designing the book's content and her production expertise. A special acknowledgment to Martha Matzke, who had the original vision for this project. Her relentless work in securing the authors and illustrator, providing historical resources, gathering information from people related to the rescue, helping secure funds, editing the story to make sure it was culturally accurate, and in many other ways was crucial to this project's completion. This book would never have been completed without Martha's valuable help.

Text copyright Alan Elliott and Annie Kwai, 2022
Illustrations copyright Evelyn Morgan, 2022
Graphic Design and Production: Cindy Rodella-Purdy

All rights reserved under International and Pan-American Copyright Conventions. No part of this book may be reprinted or reproduced or utilized in any form or by any electronic, mechanical, or other means without permission. No portion of this book may be reproduced in any form without permission from the publisher, except as permitted by U.S. copyright law. For permissions contact: alan.elliott@gmail.com or anniequai@live.com.

SUMMARY: The story of the rescue of the future President of the United States, John F. Kennedy by Solomon Island Coastwatcher Scouts during World War II.

Publisher's Cataloging-in-Publication data

Names: Elliott, Alan C., 1952-, author. | Kwai, Anna Annie, author. | Morgan, Evelyn, illustrator.

Title: Rescuing JFK : How Solomon Islanders Rescued John F. Kennedy and the Crew of the PT-109 / written by: Alan Elliott and Annie Kwai; illustrations by: Evelyn Morgan.

Identifiers: LCCN: 2022943432 | ISBN 978-0-927523-14-1 (hardback)| ISBN 978-0-927523-12-7 (paperback) | 978-0-927523-13-4 (ebook)

Subjects: LCSH Kennedy, John F. (John Fitzgerald), 1917-1963--Military leadership--Juvenile literature. | PT-109 (Torpedo boat)--Juvenile literature. | World War, 1939-1945--Campaigns--Solomon Islands--Juvenile literature. | World War, 1939-1945--Naval operations, American--Juvenile literature. | BISAC JUVENILE NONFICTION / History / Australia & Oceania | JUVENILE NONFICTION / History / United States / 20th Century Classification: LCC D774.P8 E45 2022 | DDC 940.54/26593/1--dc23

Author website: www.alanelliott.com

Contents

1 Coastwatcher Scouts   Pg. 1

2 Collision!   Pg. 7

3 Waiting for Rescue   Pg. 17

4 Men in the Bushes   Pg. 31

5 Delivering the Message   Pg. 43

6 Arranging a Rescue   Pg. 51

7 Rescuing the PT-109 Crew   Pg. 59

8 After the Rescue   Pg. 67

SOLOMON ISLANDS

KOLOMBANGARA

Amagiri and PT-109 Collision

GIZO

ROUTE SWUM BY SURVIVORS

ROUTE OF AMAGIRI

Kennedy Island

Olasana Island

Naru Island

156.50°   156.55°

1 Coastwatcher Scouts

Two Solomon Islanders, Aaron Kumana and Biuku (bee-yoo-koo) Gasa, floated in the waves along an island shore. With only the top of their heads bobbing out of the water, they looked like floating coconuts. As long as the Japanese didn't notice them, they could watch for ship and troop movements.

Every day, scouts like Kumana and Gasa spied on enemy forces. They were part of a network called the Solomon Scouts and reported what they saw to a group called the Coastwatchers who passed the information to Americans and Allied troops. Scouts and Coastwatchers knew

their information would help save the lives of stranded Allied soldiers, sailors, and pilots. Many of the Coastwatchers were government officers, missionaries, or planters who had lived in the Solomon Islands for many years.

Hundreds of scouts risked their lives daily by helping Allied soldiers during World War II. The heroic deeds of three of these scouts, Gasa (from Pasoro), Kumana (from Rannonga), and John Kari (from Rendova), had an important effect on American history.

In November 1942, Kari helped two American airmen who had been shot down over enemy territory. He hid them in the bottom of his canoe and paddled toward the U.S. Navy base in Rendova Harbor to take them to safety. When he neared American-controlled waters, two

American patrol torpedo (PT) boats (80 feet/24 meters) sped toward his canoe. The crew of PT-109 pointed guns at him and questioned him. Kari told them he was saving two American pilots. After that, the PT boat's captain, Lieutenant (junior grade) John F. Kennedy, welcomed the airmen and Kari aboard.

Scouts Kumana and Gasa were often paired together, based on Naru Island. They stayed on Naru for a week at a time, watching for enemy activity until a new crew took their place. Late one night on August 1943, a loud explosion from somewhere in the sea woke them. The scouts thought a plane had been shot down. At dawn, they could see a large black cloud of smoke in the sky between Kolombangara and Gizo islands. A few days later, they learned that an American boat had sunk, so they knew to look out for sailors in need of rescue.

A memorial honoring Solomon Scouts and Coastwatchers was dedicated in August 2011 to commemorate the August 7, 1942 US landing on Guadalcanal. Scouts and Coastwatchers helped change the course of the Pacific War by helping the Allies win this crucial battle. US Admiral William "Bull" Halsey, commander of the South Pacific Area, said, "the Coastwatchers saved Guadalcanal and Guadalcanal saved the Pacific."

Collision!

John F. Kennedy (Jack, as they called him) grew up in Boston, Massachusetts, USA, and knew boating from childhood. After joining the navy during World War II and receiving training, he was assigned command of a PT boat in Panama. Wanting to get closer to the war's action, he asked for a transfer. As a result, he was sent to the Solomon Islands in the South Pacific.

Even though Kennedy served near some of World War II's hardest-fought battles, PT-109 saw little action at first. Everything changed on August 1, 1943.

At 1900 hours (7:00 pm) that night, PT-109 joined fourteen other patrol boats on a joint mission. They entered Blackett Strait (near Kolombangara) to find and stop Japanese destroyers from delivering men, equipment, and food to their troops.

Locating destroyers at night was like a cat and mouse game. The destroyers ran without lights and at high speed. On this particular night, clouds hid the stars, the moon, and the destroyers. The PT boat formation stretched several kilometers (miles) across the straits, searching for these ghost ships in the night.

PT-109 waited in the darkness. The crew could see nothing beyond the edge of their boat and could hear only the hum of their boat's engines. Around 2:00 am in the early morning of August 2nd, Kennedy stood in the PT boat's cockpit, peering into the thick, dark night.

Suddenly, Ensign Barney Ross sensed something large coming toward them on their right (starboard) side. "Ship at two o'clock!" he shouted.

At first, Kennedy thought it was another PT boat. Then something much larger emerged from the darkness. A destroyer! He spun the ship's wheel to turn into action and shouted, "Sound general quarters!" telling his crew to get ready for battle. Ross swung his anti-tank gun around toward the enormous hulk.

It was too late. Within seconds, the Japanese destroyer (named Amagiri) cracked into the PT boat at high speed, slicing through it.

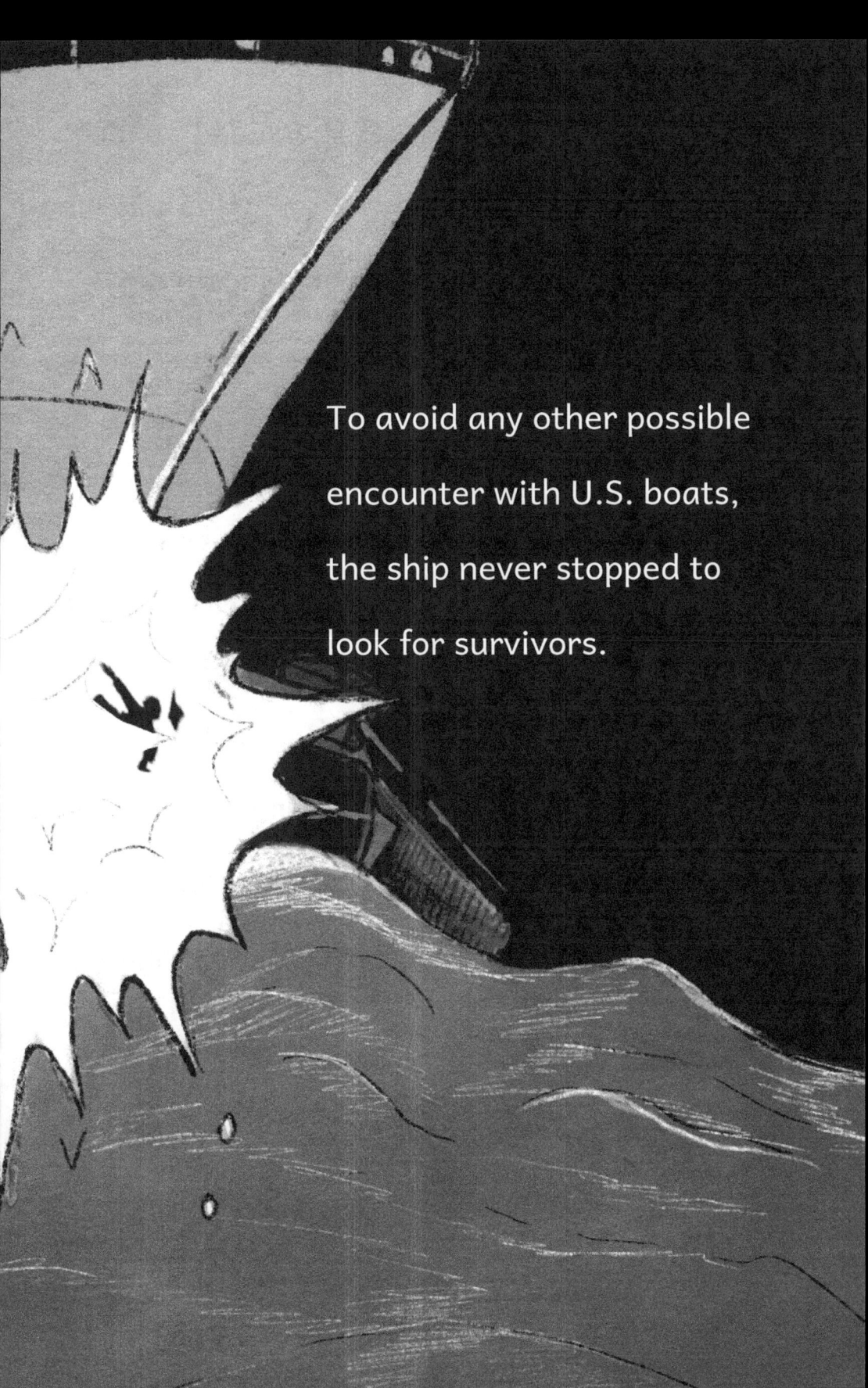

The rear hull of the PT boat (housing two large motors) ripped open in an ear-splitting cracking of metal and wood. Motor fuel spilled from ruptured tanks and caught fire, covering the sea in a blanket of flames and fumes. A giant fireball exploded into the night sky.

Only the bow (front) of the boat stayed afloat. The collision tossed Kennedy into a steel bulkhead, injuring his back. Quartermaster Edmund Mauer clung to the cockpit. Radioman John Maguire tumbled into the sea but quickly climbed back onto the bow.

The other crew members were thrown

overboard by the collision. The wake of the passing destroyer sucked them under the water. They struggled for air and popped back up into a pool of fire.

Within minutes, the lapping waves snuffed out the flaming water. Complete darkness returned. In the isolation of the open sea, no one knew who was alive and who was dead.

PT-169, the closest American boat, witnessed the explosion of PT-109. It launched two torpedoes toward the *Amagiri*. Both missed. Another boat, PT-162, also launched two torpedoes, but both failed to fire at all. Neither of the PT boat captains believed the PT-109 could have any survivors, so they turned away and returned to base.

Waiting for Rescue

As the *Amagiri* raced away, only the fifteen-foot bow (front) section of the damaged PT-109 remained afloat. The crew members who had been thrown overboard thrashed in the water, not knowing which way to swim. Motor fuel and fumes filled their stomachs and lungs. Some of

them briefly lost consciousness. If not for their life jackets, many would have drowned.

From the bow, Quartermaster Mauer shone a signal light all around to help the men in the water see the floating remains of PT-109. One by one, the men saw the signal light or heard Kennedy calling to them and swam or were towed by one of the other sailors toward the boat.

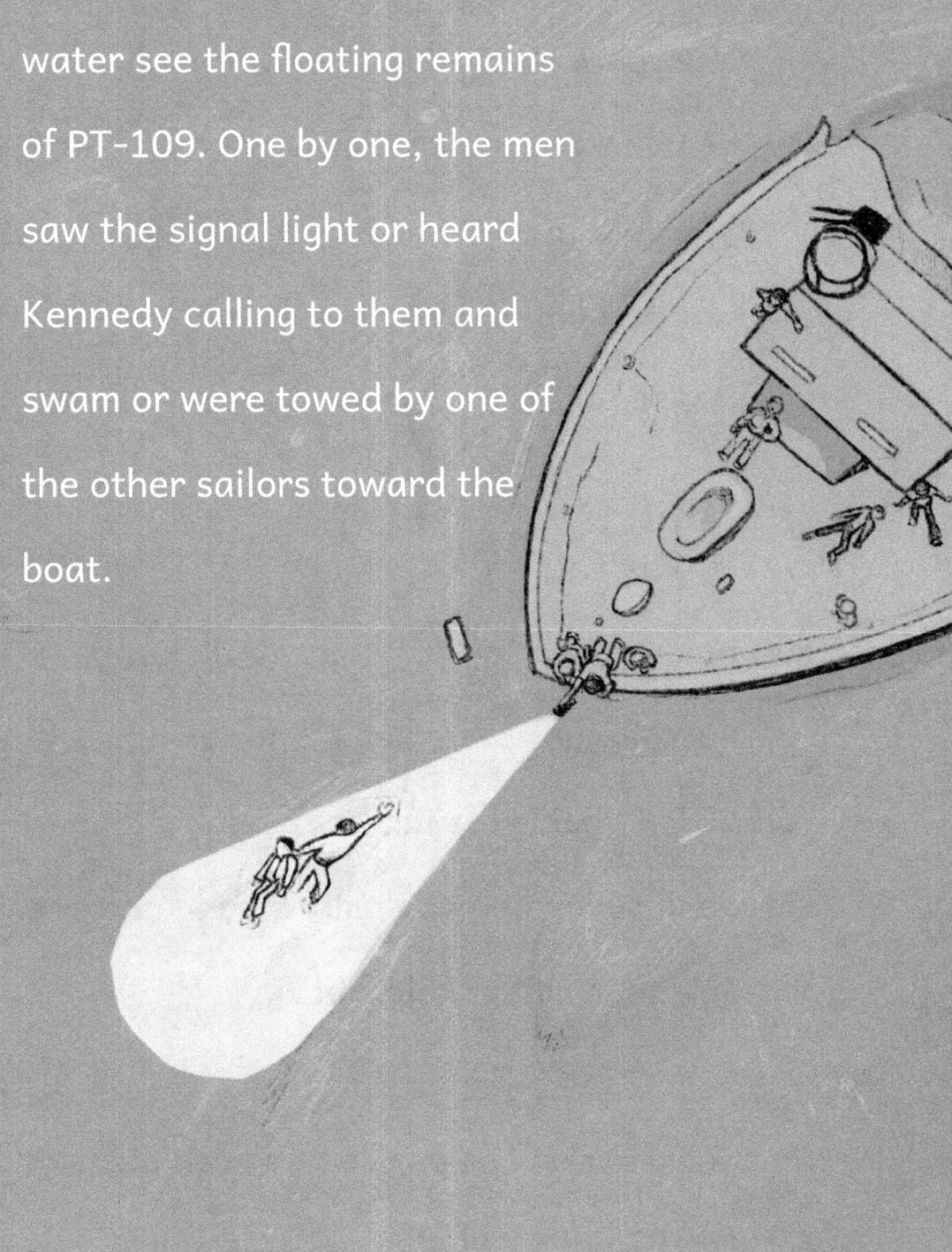

From somewhere in the darkness, Kennedy heard the voice of Gunner Charles Harris, "Mr. Kennedy. Mr. Kennedy, McMahon is badly hurt!" Kennedy jumped into the water toward Harris's voice and found them.

"I'm kind of burnt," said McMahon. In fact, he couldn't move his arms or hands at all. Kennedy dragged McMahon towards the boat using the strap on McMahon's life jacket. It took a long hard time of swimming against a strong current to get McMahon to the ship's bow.

In time, eleven crew members gathered at the part of the PT boat still afloat. Two sailors,

Motor Machinist's Mate Harold William Marney and Torpedoman's Mate Andrew Kirksey, were never seen again.

PT109 Crew in August 1943

Captain - John F. "Jack" Kennedy
Seaman - Raymond Albert
Gunner's Mate - Charles A. "Bucky" Harris
Motor Machinist - William Johnston.
Torpedoman's Mate - Andrew Jackson Kirksey
Radioman - John E. Maguire
Motor Machinist's Mate - Harold William Marney
Quartermaster (and cook) - Edgar E. Mauer
Motor Machinist's Mate - Patrick H. "Pappy" McMahon
Ensign - George H. R. "Barney" Ross
Torpedoman's Mate - Ray L. Starkey
Ensign - Leonard J. Thom
Motor Machinist's Mate - Gerard E. Zinser

The crew waited through the night and into the morning. They knew some other PT boat would have seen the explosion, but no American rescue boat ever arrived. They wondered what they would to do if the Japanese found them first. Surely the enemy had seen the explosion. Would they fight? Or surrender? Little by little, the bow sank lower in the water. After twelve hours, and with no rescue in sight, Kennedy took action.

Several islands loomed near them, but Kennedy knew most were occupied by enemy troops. The nearest American base was sixty kilometers (thirty-eight miles) away at Rendova Harbor.

A dot of an island (named Plum Pudding) about five and a half kilometers (three and a half miles) away looked too small to have enemy troops, so they swam toward it. By gripping McMahon's life vest strap in his teeth and swimming toward the island, Kennedy managed to drag McMahon along with him through the water. Other crew members clung to wooden planks as they splashed their way through the waves.

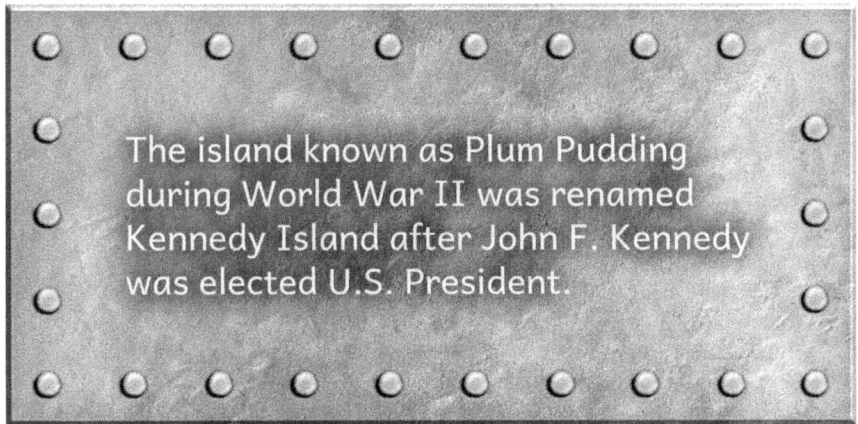

The island known as Plum Pudding during World War II was renamed Kennedy Island after John F. Kennedy was elected U.S. President.

All of the men knew these waters were famous for man-eating sharks that liked to feast on shipwrecked sailors. Even saltwater crocodiles were known to hunt here. If attacked by either the Japanese or sea creatures, the crew members had no protection. So they kept swimming.

After four exhausting hours, Kennedy, McMahon, and Mauer were the first to reach the small island. The coral near the beach bruised and cut their feet as they pulled themselves onto the shore. Both were so tired they could only crawl about a meter (a few feet) onto the beach before they collapsed in exhaustion.

The other crew members arrived soon after. Many of them vomited saltwater as they pulled themselves onto dry land. Kennedy had everyone hide under bushes near the beach.

Within minutes, they heard the thumpa, thumpa, thump of an enemy barge propeller. The Japanese barge floated by the island less than a hundred yards away. Were the troops on the barge making a normal delivery, or looking for them? Kennedy and his men froze in place. They knew if they were spotted, they would be captured – or killed.

After gaining strength, a few men explored the island - an area a little larger than a football field. At a different time, the island could have been a picnic spot for Americans. Colorful parrots and hornbills fluttered here and there in the dense foliage. Crabs scampered along the white sandy beach, and waves gurgled in the reef near the shore. But this was no holiday for the soldiers. They had to make sure the island was safe. Luckily, no enemy outposts were found. Not so lucky was their search for freshwater – there was none. The men found a few fallen coconuts and tried to eat them, but they were sour and gave the crew stomach aches. To add to their misery, the crew had to fend off millions of pesky mosquitoes.

Even though Kennedy was exhausted, he decided to swim several kilometers (miles) into Ferguson Passage that night, hoping to signal a passing American boat. It helped that he'd been on the Harvard University swimming team. When no ships appeared, Kennedy swam back to Plum Pudding. For the next few nights, he and Ensign George Ross took turns swimming in search of rescue boats. They spotted nothing. Still, they did not give up.

On August 4, Kennedy had his men swim three kilometers (about two miles) to another island, Olasana, hoping to find water and food. This island was no better than Plum Pudding but was a little closer to Ferguson Passage.

The next day, Kennedy and Ross swam another kilometer (about a half-mile) to a third island, Naru. There, they found a little hope: a wrecked Japanese barge. Near it, they found some Japanese candy and a tin of water. They ate and drank the treasure.

Then they heard voices.

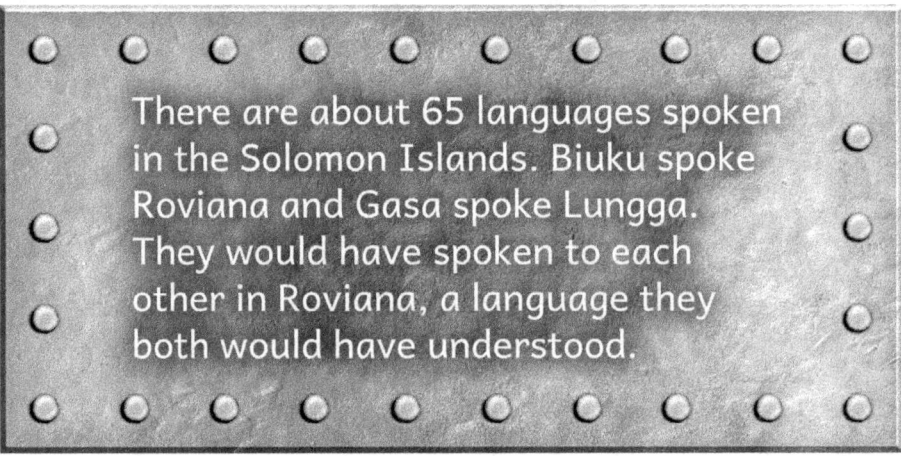
There are about 65 languages spoken in the Solomon Islands. Biuku spoke Roviana and Gasa spoke Lungga. They would have spoken to each other in Roviana, a language they both would have understood.

Men in Bushes

Early in the afternoon on August 5, Scouts Kumana and Gasa were paddling around Naru Island on one of their daily patrols, looking for enemy activity when they saw the bow of a wrecked Japanese barge rested along the shore. Anchoring their canoe on the reef, they swam to the beach. Boxes, clothes, cooking utensils, and

rifles littered the area around the wreckage.

While picking through the plunder, Kumana saw two men farther down on the beach. Thinking the men were Japanese, Kumana said, "*Yumi go.*" ("Let's go.") They swam back to their canoe and paddled away.

Back in the safety of the sea, Gasa grew thirsty. Since Olasana Island was nearby, they decided to go there and drink a coconut.

As they approached the shore, a large man stepped onto the beach and called to them, "Come help. I'm an American."

Gasa understood a little English, and he yelled back, "*No, yu Japani.*" ("No, you are Japanese.")

The man pulled up his sleeve and showed his arm, "Look at my skin. It's white."

Gasa still didn't believe him. He said, (It doesn't matter if your skin is white, you are still Japanese.) "*No mata yu waet skin, yu Japani!*"

Kumana told Gasa the man was too large to be an American. He must be German, helping the Japanese. (The man was

Ensign Thom, a muscular former football player.)

Kumana and Gasa kept talking to Thom, but they didn't understand most of what he said. After a while, another man came from behind the bushes. He said, "Do you know John Kari from Rendova?"

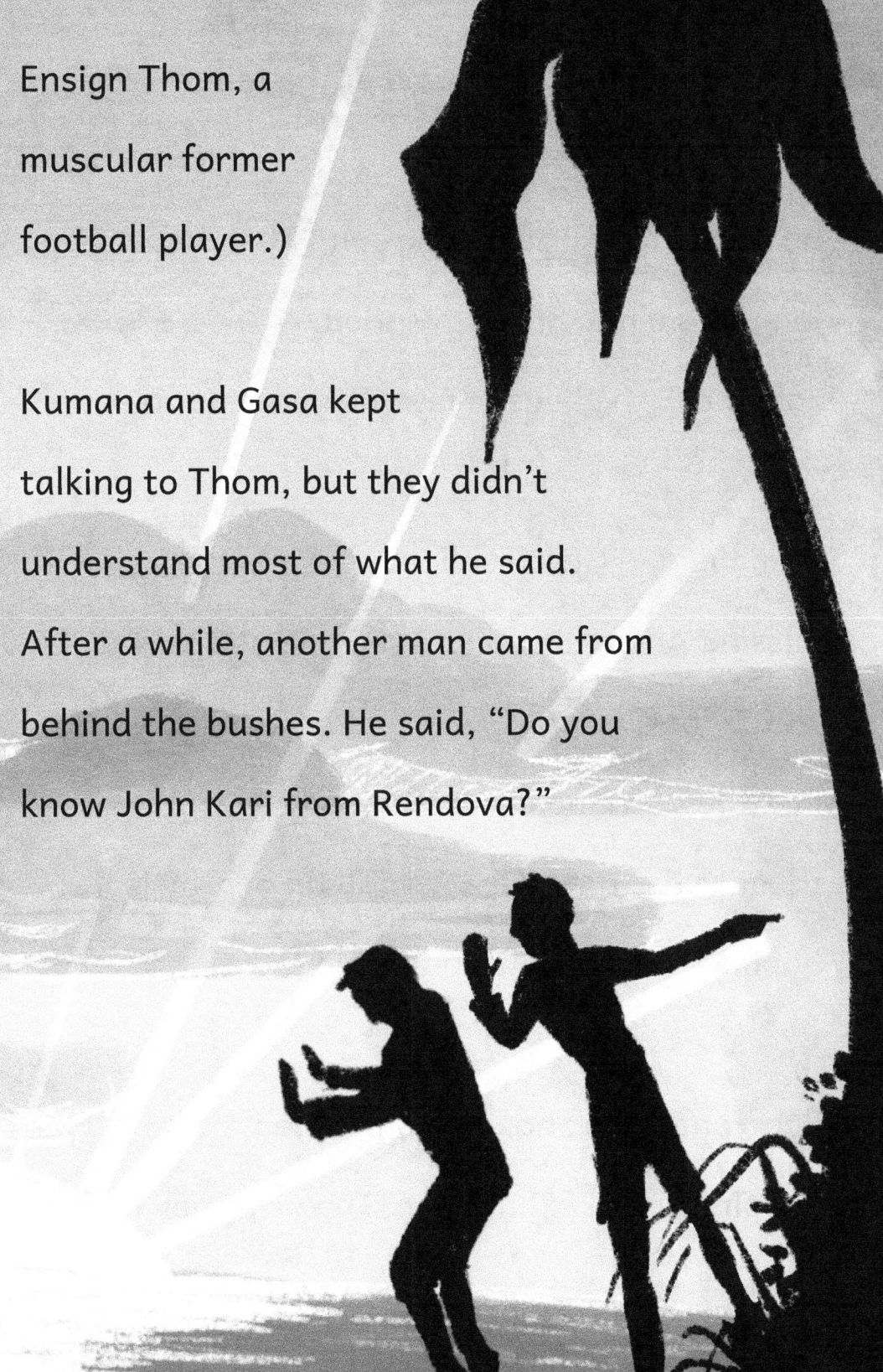

Gasa recognized the name of the fellow scout. Since only an American would know John Kari, he said, "Ya, mi save long John Kari. Hemi stap long ples blong mi long Madou." ("Yes, I know John Kari - he lives in my village at Madou.")

Kumana and Gasa realized these were the missing American sailors they'd been told to watch for earlier. The scouts came ashore and met the crew members. Kennedy was not with them at the time. He was still on nearby Naru, hoping to signal a friendly ship.

Everyone shook hands. Some cried from happiness and exhaustion, knowing they'd been found.

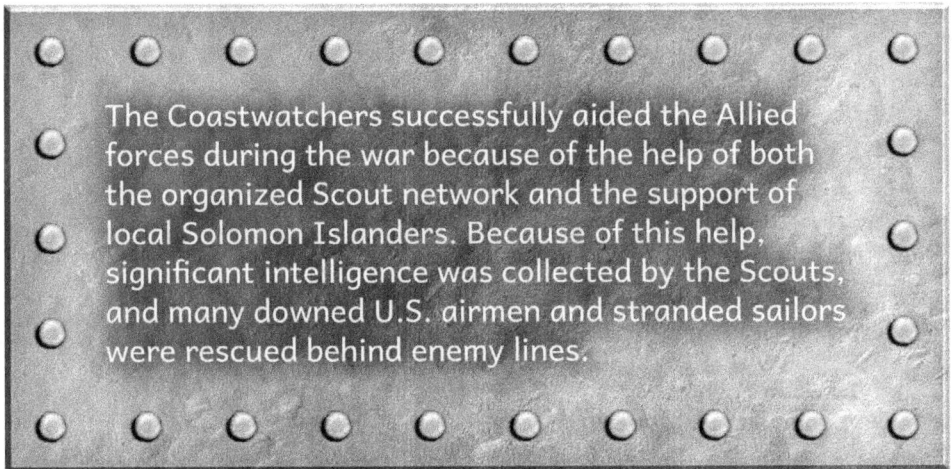

The Coastwatchers successfully aided the Allied forces during the war because of the help of both the organized Scout network and the support of local Solomon Islanders. Because of this help, significant intelligence was collected by the Scouts, and many downed U.S. airmen and stranded sailors were rescued behind enemy lines.

However, they were still in danger because the scouts had no way of getting the crew off the island. The sailors had only survived by licking a little dew off of leaves. If they couldn't get food, water, and medical help soon, they would die of injuries, starvation, or thirst. One crew member was in immediate need of medical help. To keep the badly burned Pat McMahon as safe and comfortable as possible, the other crew members had dug a hole in the sand to make a cool place for him to rest.

Gasa gave the hungry crew a few yams that they had in their canoe. Although welcomed, the food was only enough to fend off starvation for a little while. Ensign Thom asked the scouts to take him to Rendova in their canoe to arrange a rescue, but he was too big for their small canoe.

Instead, Kumana and Gasa stayed with the men into the night, talking as best they could about making a rescue plan. Around midnight, the men heard Captain Kennedy calling from the sea. The crew answered him, "We're saved. Two locals have found us."

As Kennedy came into camp and saw Kumana and Gasa, he realized they were the same two he'd seen on Naru. He put his arms around them, and since he knew some of the Solomon Islands Pijin language, he could talk to them.

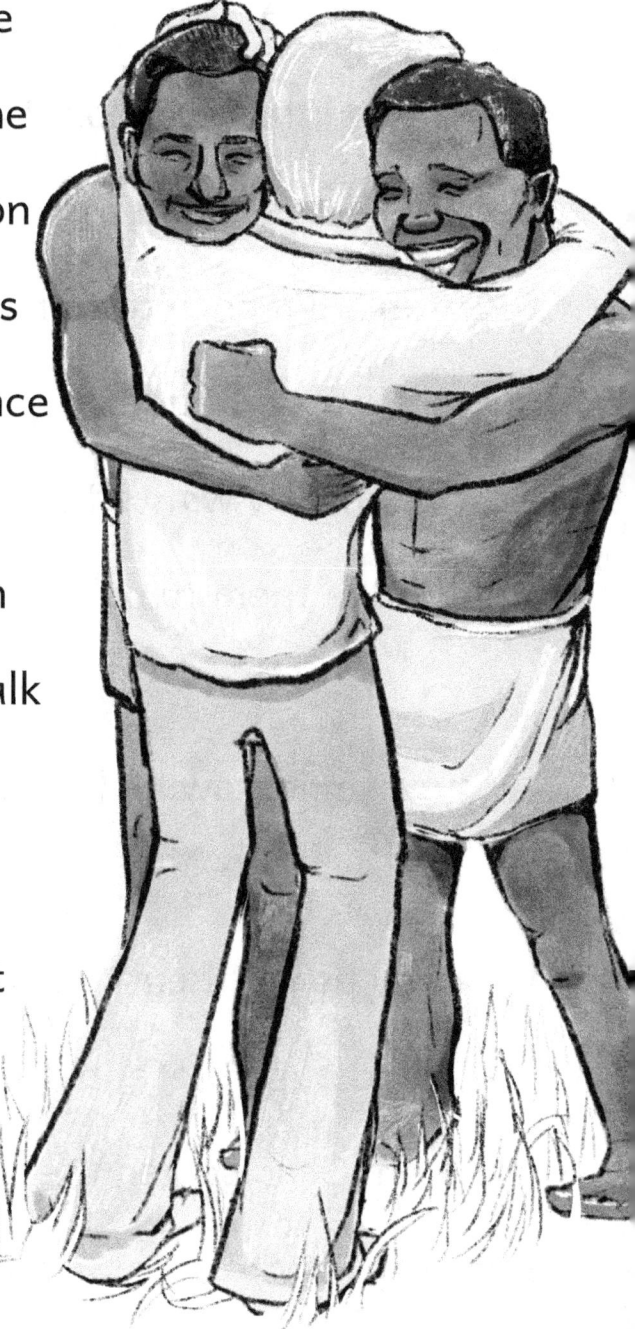

Kennedy still thought their best bet for rescue was finding a passing American ship. He asked the scouts to take him back to Naru so he could keep swimming into Ferguson Passage. They hid Kennedy under palm fronds in their canoe as they took him back to Naru in case an enemy plane flew overhead. Once they were back on Naru, Kennedy wanted to know how long it would take them to paddle to Rendova.

"Maybe tomorrow night," said Gasa.

Kennedy asked them to take a message to the Allied base there, but he had no paper to write on. Gasa solved the problem. He showed Kennedy how to scratch a note on the coconut

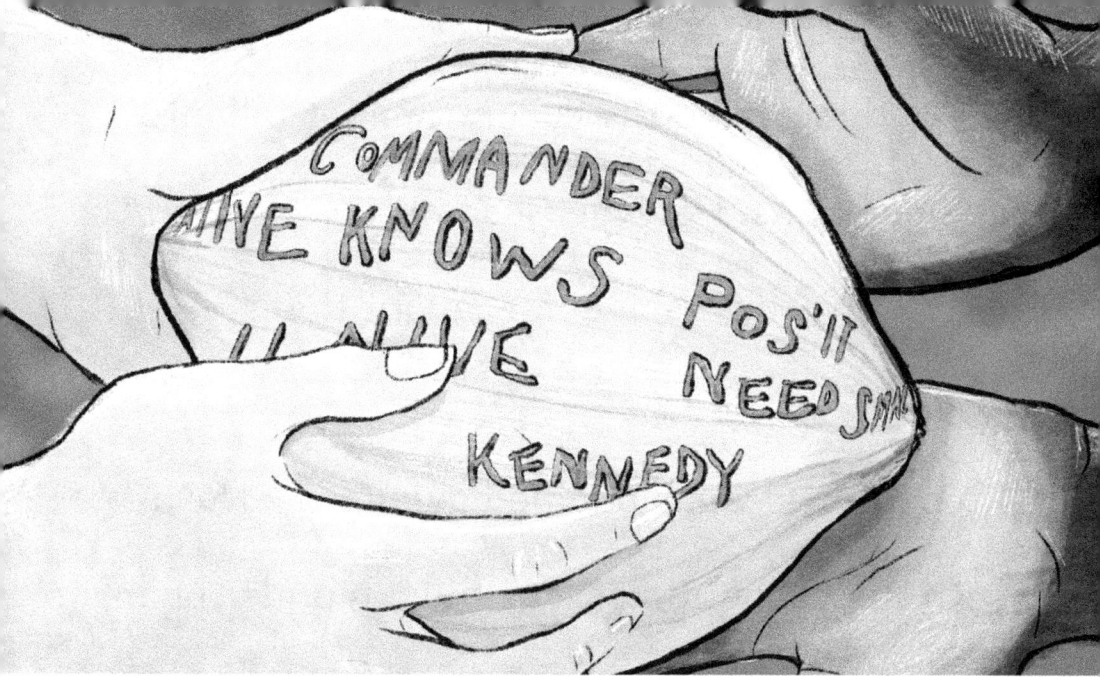

husk. Kennedy wrote a message saying the scouts knew the missing sailor's position (POS'IT.)

"NAURO ISL... COMMANDER... NATIVE KNOWS POS'IT... HE CAN PILOT... 11 ALIVE... NEED SMALL BOAT... KENNEDY."

Kennedy worried the coconut might fall into enemy hands. He gave Gasa his knife to scratch out the words if someone caught them.

Kumana and Gasa paddled away from Naru with the coconut message hidden under palm leaves in their canoe. They stopped on Olasana to tell the other men the plan. Ensign Lenny Thom found a small scrap of paper and wrote a second rescue message, and gave it to the scouts. The fate of the PT-109 crew depended on the scouts paddling their small canoe across the open sea in a war zone to deliver their two messages to the Americans.

Delivering the Messages

Salty ripples followed every stroke of their paddles as Kumana and Gasa's canoe eased away from Olasana and into the open sea. Their coconut-frond sail fluttered in the wind and rain. The cloud cover protected them from the eyes of enemy planes.

Eleven kilometers (about seven miles) into their sixty-one kilometer (thirty-eight mile) canoe journey, Kumana and Gasa pulled ashore on Parara Island's white sand beach in Vonavona lagoon. Once there, they told Benjamin Kevu, a clerk for the scouts, about finding the PT-109 crew alive. They showed him the messages.

Kevu took action. He told Kumana and Gasa where to get a larger canoe for the rest of their journey. He also told them to take fellow scout John Kari with them because he spoke better English. At about 6:00 pm that night, the three scouts headed across the sea toward the American base at Rendova Harbor.

Kevu also sent the news to Coastwatcher Reg Evans, who operated a radio post deep in the jungle. However, Evans' radio needed work, so he couldn't send a message to the U.S. headquarters telling them the PT-109 crew was alive and had been found. It would take until the morning to fix it.

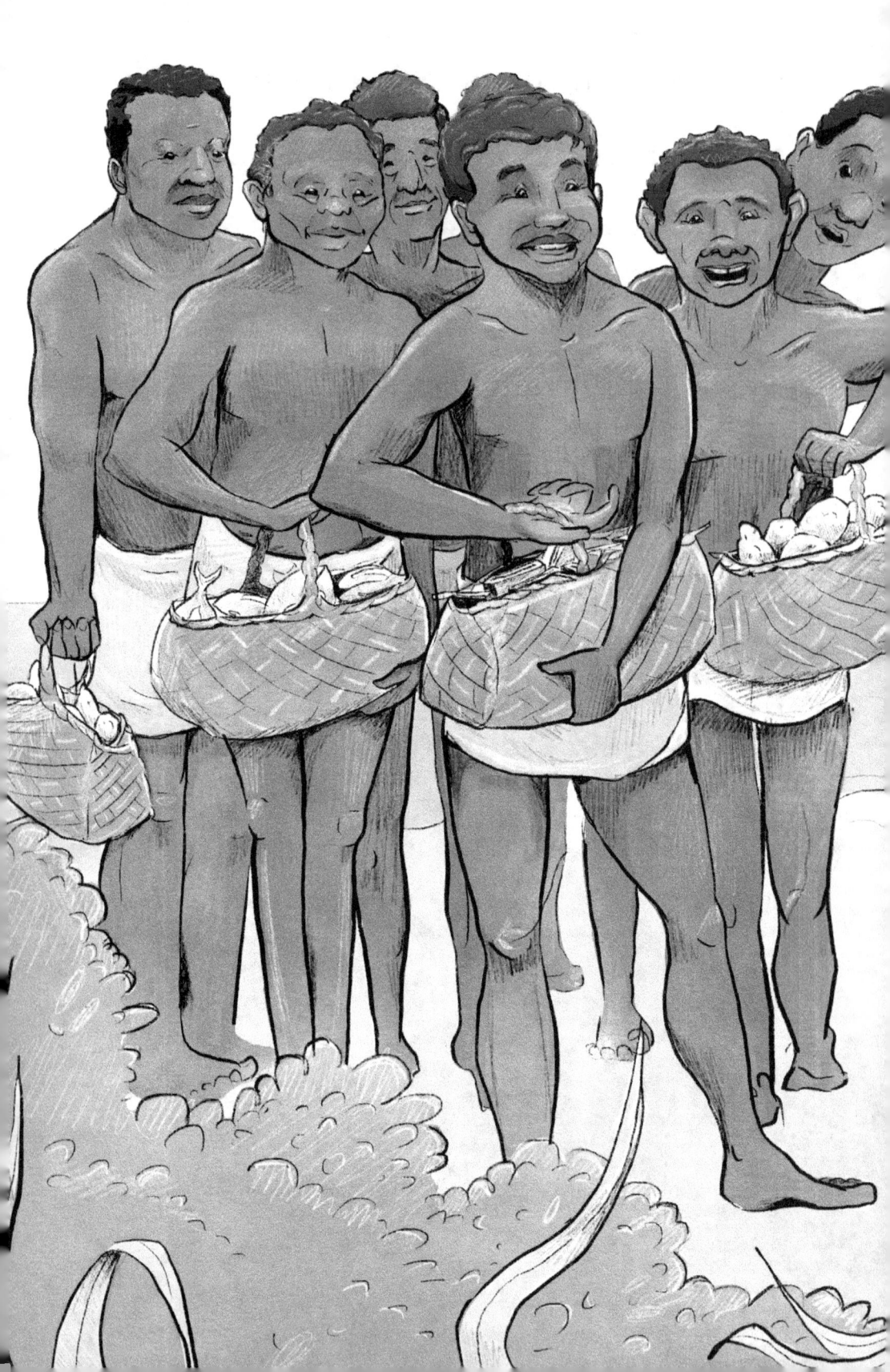

While waiting for the radio, Evans sent seven of his scouts to Olasana. They loaded their canoes with yams, rice, sweet potatoes, fish, roast beef hash, a portable stove, and water. Evans also sent a letter to Kennedy advising him to come to Parara with the scouts to plan a final rescue. When the canoes arrived on Olasana, the famished PT-109 crew celebrated their first real food in six days.

After the feast, Kennedy returned to the

Coastwatchers hideout. Like Kumana and Gasa had done before, the islanders hid him under palm fronds. Once in the open sea, they heard the drone of enemy fighters overhead. The planes approached and circled the canoes.

Kennedy shouted, "What's going on?"

"Stap kuaet," (stay quiet) said the scouts.

After some discussion, the scouts waved at the pilots, acting as friendly as they could. The fighters turned and continued on their mission. Once the planes were out of sight, the scouts sang a hymn in thankfulness to God.

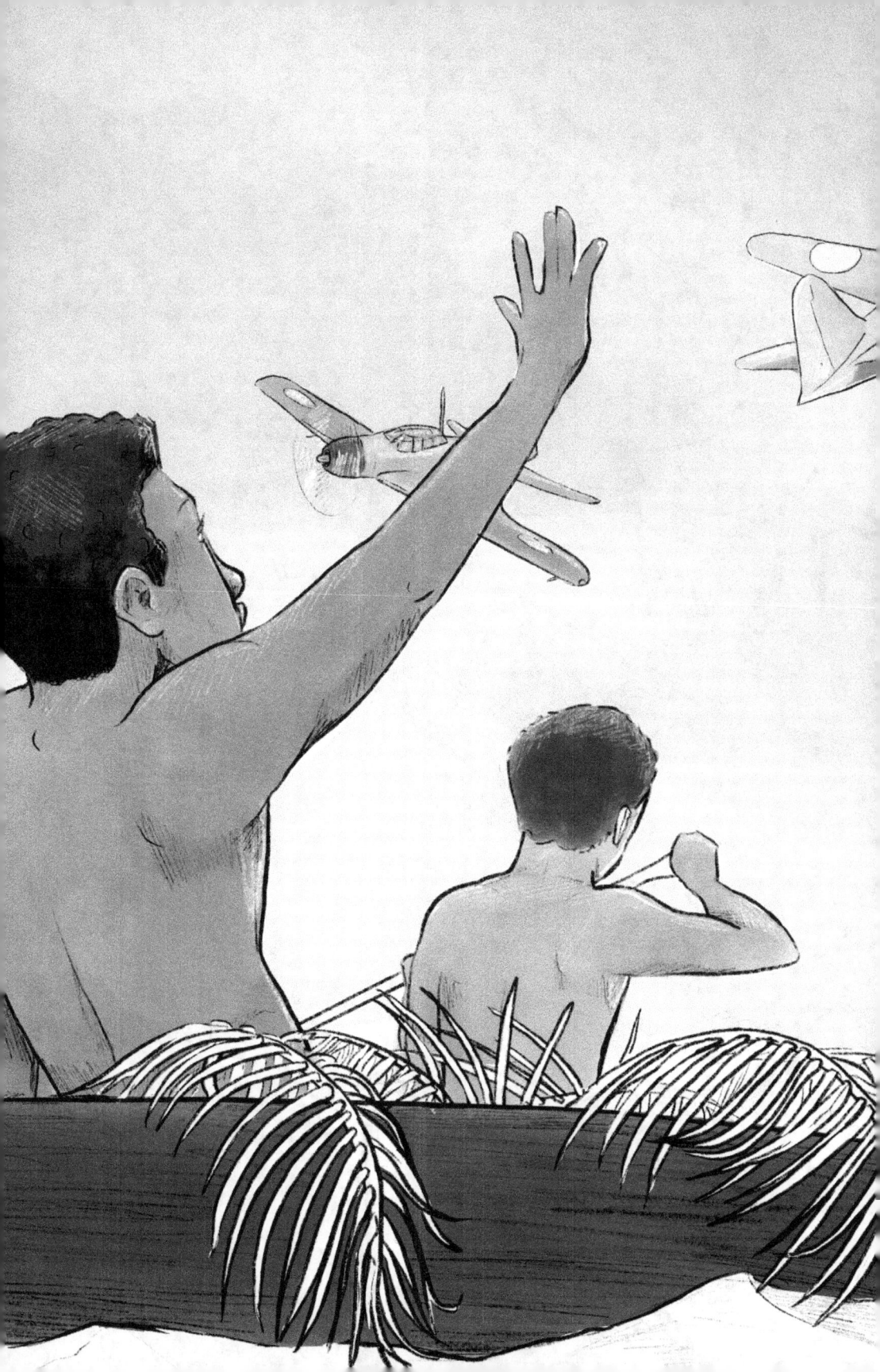

Arranging the Rescue

Kilometers (miles) away, Kumana, Gasa, and Kari arrived at a U.S. military outpost at Roviana Island off the island of New Georgia. The base swarmed with activity. Trucks, big guns, and ammunition were scattered among the palm trees. Wounded and dead soldiers from a recent battle covered the dock.

The scouts showed Kennedy's coconut and Thom's letter to some soldiers. They were taken to see Army Colonel George Hill.

With the help of an officer who spoke some Pijin, Gasa told Hill, "Americans stranded on island behind the [Japanese]." And "give him rescue boat immediately." The scouts pointed to a map, showing the PT crew's location. Hill had never heard of Kennedy and wasn't sure what to make of the scout's story. He sent a message to the Intelligence Section asking for information.

Meanwhile, the scouts waited.

Gasa felt "crazy, not knowing what else to do." He held the coconut message in one hand and waved a machete in the other, saying, "Bot wea? Man ya hemi siki!" ("Where's the boat? The man is sick.")

At 2:00 pm, Hill received information that a radio message from Coastwatcher Reg Evans (whose radio had been fixed) had confirmed the scouts' story. Now convinced the news was real, Hill sent the three scouts by boat to the Navy outpost at Rendova to arrange a rescue.

On Saturday, August 7, the three Solomon Island Scouts arrived at the Rendova Harbor PT Boat Base. Gasa handed the coconut message to Lieutenant "Bud" Liebenow, who quickly showed it to Base Commander Thomas Warfield.

When Warfield saw the coconut message, he questioned the scouts. "Who wrote this?"

"Captain Kennedy," said Gasa.

"Who showed him how to do this with the coconut?"

"I did," said Gasa.

Warfield had been assured there were no PT-109 survivors. He wondered if this could be a trick to lure his PT boats into an ambush. And yet, three messages verified the scout's story – the coconut, the scribbled note from Ensign Thom, and the radio dispatch from Reg Evans.

Warfield decided to risk one PT boat for

the trip, Liebenow's PT-157. Through the Coastwatchers radio network, Liebenow arranged to pick up Kennedy near Patparan Island, and then his crew on Olasana. Since the rescue would happen at night, and enemy boats might be in the area, they agreed on four gunshots as a signal to verify each other's identity.

At 7:00 pm that night, PT-157 left Rendova. The boat zigzagged across the sea to protect it from being tracked by enemy gunners. Several other people joined the rescue team, including two newspaper reporters, Frank Hewlett and Leif Erickson.

Kumana, Gasa, and Kari were given a chance to stay behind since the trip might be dangerous. They answered, "Hem oreat nomoa. Sapos olketa dae, bae yumi dae wetem olketa." ("It's ok. If they die, we die, too.")

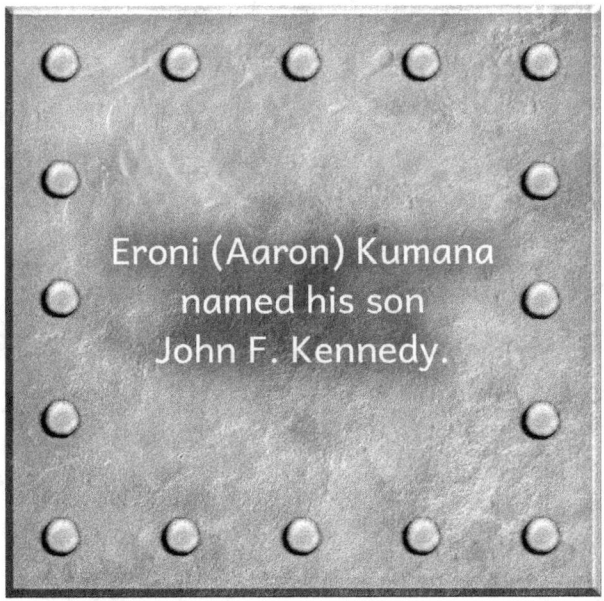

Eroni (Aaron) Kumana named his son John F. Kennedy.

7. Rescuing the PT-109 Crew

PT-157's speed surprised the scouts, and the whump, whump, whump as the boat bounced across the waves made Kumana and Gasa seasick for most of the trip. They had never been on such a fast boat before.

After four hours of zigzagging, they arrived at the pickup point. Captain Liebenow fired four shots in the air. Kennedy, waiting in an islander's canoe, responded with three shots from his pistol. With his gun out of ammunition, Kennedy picked up a rifle and fired a final fourth shot. Its recoil almost knocked him overboard.

Kennedy's canoe pulled up beside PT-157. John Kari reached out his hand and helped Kennedy climb aboard, saying (in his formal British accent), "Good evening, Lieutenant Kennedy." After a round of hugs with his rescuers, Kennedy joined Captain Liebenow in the cockpit. They pointed the boat toward Olasana.

As they approached the island, Kari and other crew members boarded a small boat attached to PT-157 and guided it through the island's shallow reefs. Soon after midnight, PT-157 edged up to the Olasana shore.

The exhausted PT-109 crew woke to Kennedy's shouts. They were given water and food, and medics checked them for injury. They took the most badly wounded man, Pat McMahon, aboard first, and the others followed.

During the trip back to base, the weary and weakened Kennedy broke down and cried as he thought of his two crew members that didn't make it back alive. Other members of the rescued crew celebrated with drinks, laughter, and song. Motor Machinist William Johnston put his arms around Kumana and Gasa and led everyone in a Christian chorus:

Jesus loves me, this I know,

For the Bible tells me so.

Little ones to Him belong,

They are weak, but He is strong.

Yes, Jesus loves me … the Bible tells me so.

PT-157 docked at Rendova at 5:15 am. Friends greeted the PT-109 crew at the dock with handshakes and a breakfast feast. The most severely wounded were taken to a hospital. Kennedy sat at a table with Kumana, Gasa, and Kari, telling them, "Thank you for saving my life and the lives of my crew. If I'm alive at the end of the war, I'll come to see you."

Most of Kennedy's crew continued to serve in the Navy for the rest of the war. The reporters, who had witnessed the rescue, sent their stories to their newspapers, and John F. Kennedy's name made headlines all over the United States.

Kumana, Gasa, and Kari returned to their duties as scouts, helping the Coastwatchers. They sometimes wondered if they would ever hear from Jack Kennedy again, as he promised.

> In recognition of Solomon Island Scouts, President Barack Obama said the following, "I am pleased to join in honoring the tremendous contributions Coastwatchers and Solomon Scouts made to the cause of freedom during World War II. Their efforts helped save the Pacific, and they are worthy of the highest praise and recognition." (July 23, 2012)

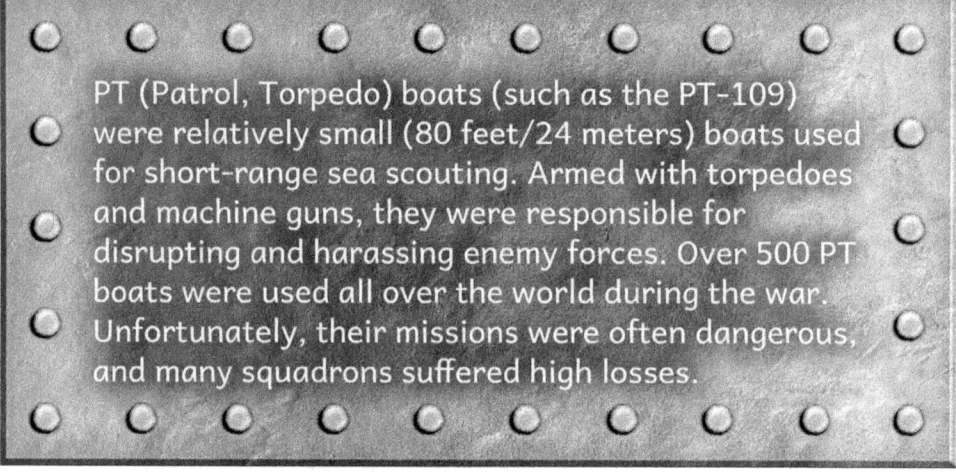

PT (Patrol, Torpedo) boats (such as the PT-109) were relatively small (80 feet/24 meters) boats used for short-range sea scouting. Armed with torpedoes and machine guns, they were responsible for disrupting and harassing enemy forces. Over 500 PT boats were used all over the world during the war. Unfortunately, their missions were often dangerous, and many squadrons suffered high losses.

After the Rescue

Kennedy could have returned to the U.S. after being rescued, but he chose to take command of another boat, PT-59. Soon however, his back injuries became so bad he had to go to the United States for treatment.

The war ended in September 1945.

From newspapers, magazines, and newsreels, everyone in the United States heard about Jack Kennedy's dramatic rescue. His fame helped him win a 1947 election to the U.S. Congress and the Senate in 1953. In 1960, he was elected President of the United States. As president, John F. Kennedy (often called "JFK") wrote about the scouts, "If it weren't for these two who saved me at Naru, I wouldn't be here today." Kennedy always kept the coconut husk with its carved message on his desk at the White House to remind him of the way the Solomon Islands scouts had rescued him. He meant to keep his promise and return to the Solomon Islands and find Kumana, Gasa, and Kari, but sadly President Kennedy was assassinated in 1963 before he had the chance.

The two scouts were disappointed they never saw Kennedy again. However, in 2002, JFK's nephew, Max Kennedy, came to the Solomon Islands and met Kumana and Gasa. He brought a letter from John Kennedy's youngest brother Edward "Ted" that thanked them again for their heroism. When Max put his hand on 83-year-old Kumana's shoulder, he said, "Thank you so much." Kumana cried happy tears as they hugged each other.

Eroni "Aaron" Kumana, Biuku Gasa, and John Kari are no longer living. However, an exhibit at the John F. Kennedy Presidential Library and Museum in Boston, Massachusetts, remembers them as heroes. Solomon Islands Scouts that risked their lives during the war will forever be celebrated for their bravery and courage and how they shaped the course of U.S. history.

People associated with the rescue of John F. Kennedy include:

- Eroni (Aaron) Kumana, Coastwatcher Scout from Rannonga (rescuer)
- Biuku Gasa, Coastwatcher Scout from Pasoro (rescuer)
- John Kari, Coastwatcher Scout from Rendova (helped during the rescue)
- Benjamin Kevu, a clerk for the Coastwather Scouts (helped during the rescue)
- Reg Evans, Coastwatcher and radio operator (helped during the rescue)
- Thomas Warfield, Commander PT Boat Base
- Lieutenant "Bud" Liebenow, PT-157 Boat Captain that rescued the PT-109 crew
- Many other Solomon Island based Coastwatchers and Scouts contributed to the Royal Australian Navy's Coastwatcher network that saved JFK. In fact, the Australian government awarded over 500 medals to honor Solomon Island Coastwatchers and Scouts for their service during World War II.

Timeline

April 5, 1905: Birth of John Zirugumi Kari.

May 29, 1917: Birth of John F. Kennedy in Brookline, Massachusetts.

circa 1919: Birth of Eroni (Aaron) Kumana in the Western Province of the Solomon Islands.

1922: A coast watching organization is created by the Australian Commonwealth Naval Board.

July 27, 1923: Birth of Biuku Gasa in the Western Province of the Solomon Islands.

September 1939: Outbreak of World War II (1939-45) in Europe.

December 7, 1941: Japanese bomb Pearl Harbor, compelling the U.S. to enter World War II.

January 1942: Japanese begin an invasion of Solomon Islands.

June 1942: Coastwatchers become part of the Allies' southwest Pacific command.

August 7, 1942: U.S troops land on Guadalcanal and Tulagi.

1942-43: John F. Kennedy takes command of PT-109 (a U.S. Motor Torpedo Boat) in the South Pacific.

1943: Aaron Kumana (age 24) and Biuku Gasa (age 19) join the Coastwatchers.

August 2, 1943 (Monday):
- PT-109 patrols in Blackett Strait along with fourteen other PT boats.
- About 2:15 am in the morning, PT-109 is rammed by a Japanese destroyer named the *Amagiri*.
- PT-109 splits in half. Two crewmen are killed.
- Gasoline spills into the ocean and erupts in flames.
- The bow of the boat remains afloat.
- Kennedy is thrown against the cockpit, hurting his back.

- All survivors aboard the damaged boat abandon it, thinking it might sink any moment. They call for the other survivors in the darkness. Kennedy, Thom, and Ross swim out to survivors and bring them back toward the boat. This took three hours. Eleven survivors are gathered.
- Later that morning, since the bow hasn't sunk, the survivors get back onto the remains of the boat, hoping a rescue ship will soon come.
- In the afternoon, Kennedy and his surviving crew decide to swim to an uninhabited island, Plum Pudding, about five and a half kilometers (three and a half miles) away.

August 3-5, 1943: Kennedy and Ross swim into the Ferguson Passage hoping to flag down an American ship. They see none.

August 5, 1943: Kumana and Gasa see Kennedy and Ross on Naru Island, but think they are Japanese and leave.

August 6, 1943: Kennedy returns to Olasana Island and discovers that Eroni and Biuku had made contact with the remaining PT-109 crew.

August 7, 1943: Kennedy returns to Naru, and Ross swims back to Olasana. Kennedy sends scouts with a message to get help at the Allied base. Kumana and Gasa let other Coastwatchers in Vonavona know of the survivors on Olasana. Seven Coastwatchers from Vonavona bring food and water to the survivors on Olasana.

August 8, 1943: Scouts arrive at an Army base on Roviana Island, and have a hard time convincing Army Colonel George Hill of PT-109 survivors. Finally, the scouts' message is believed and they are sent to the Navy base at Rendova and PT-157 is sent to rescue PT-109 survivors.

March 1, 1945: JFK is discharged from the Navy.

November 8, 1960: JFK is elected President of the United States

November 22, 1963: JFK is assassinated.

July 10, 2002: Robert Ballard discovers the location of PT-109.

November 2002: Max Kennedy visits Biuku and Eroni (Aaron) in the Solomon Islands. Edward "Ted" Kennedy says in a letter, that his brother Jack "often spoke of the great courage of those who came to his aid."

November 23, 2005: Biuku Gasa dies, age 82

August 2, 2014: Eroni Kumana dies, age 95

References and Further Reading:
Abraham, Philip, John F. Kennedy and PT109, Rosen Book Words, 2002.
Laracy, Hugh, and White, Geoffrey (editors). "Oral Accounts from Solomon Islanders" (Eroni "Aaron" Kumana, Biuku Gasa, and John Kari) O'O', A Journal of Solomon Islands Studies Number 4, 1988.

Kennedy, Max, video of a visit with Gasa and Kumana, 2002. (Link October 20, 2020)

Donovan, Robert J. PT 109, John F. Kennedy in WW II, MJF books, 2001.

Doyle, William, PT 109: An American Epic of War, Survival, and the Destiny of John F. Kennedy, William Morrow, 2015.

Kwai, Anna Annie. (2017). Solomon Islanders in World War II : an Indigenous perspective. Acton, ACT: ANU Press

Author Notes:

This story features two types of boats: a canoe and a patrol torpedo boat. Many people in the Solomon Islands live along the coast. Thus, dugout canoes are quite common and provide a way to move from village to village, for fishing, to and from a market, or even to school or church. In this story, Eroni Kumana and Biuku Gasa would have been traveling in a dugout canoe, perhaps even one they had made themselves! When a skilled canoe builder wants to make a new canoe, they go to the bush and look for a special kind of tree; Gmelina Qoliti (or white beech.) These trees grow straight and tall, and the wood is light enough to float. Once a suitable tree is found, it is chopped down and left to dry out for a month or so. One tall tree can be used to make 2 or 3 canoes. The canoe builder returns to the tree and carves the canoe shape with an adz. The inside of the canoe is also dug out. When the canoe has been roughly carved out, the carver ties ropes around it and drags the canoe to the sea. The canoe can then be towed behind a canoe to the village.

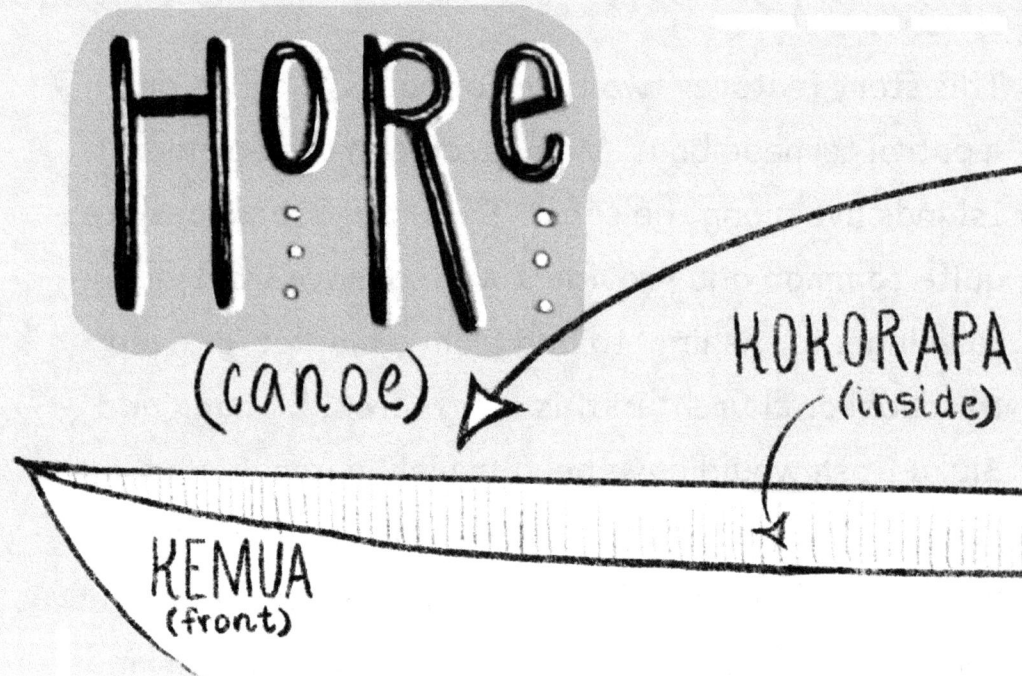

TATAVA (back)

For more information scan QR Code

To ensure the canoe is strong and doesn't split in two, a couple of pieces of wood are carved to fit inside the canoe near the front and back.

(CUT AWAY VIEW OF THE CANOE)

The builder continues to carve the canoe into the right shape and ensures it is balanced. The sides of the canoe should all be the same thickness. Paddles are carved out of a strong hardwood like vasa. The canoe illustrated here is the type used by Solomon Islanders during the time of this story.

The other boat featured in the story is a patrol torpedo boat (PT boat) used by the U.S. Navy during World War II. This boat is about 24 meters (80 feet) long. It was a reasonably inexpensive boat made of metal and wood. These boats were nimble and quick, although not very well suited for combat. Some were converted into gunboats and used to patrol enemy waters, hunt for enemy warships and transport ships, and so on. However, their record of success in action was not outstanding. Often their torpedoes did not fire correctly or did not explode on impact. Nevertheless, the boats were helpful in patrolling enemy waters and rescuing stranded sailors. The boats supported a crew of about 12-17 sailors. The illustration shows many of the features of a typical PT boat, such as the PT-109 commanded by Lieutenant Kennedy.

A Brief History of the Solomon Islands Related to WW II

The Solomon Islands are made up of over 900 islands, scattered over an area of approximately 28,000 square kilometers (11,157 sq mi) in the South Pacific, northeast of Australia. About 500,000 people live there. The capital is Honiara.

The Solomon Islands were first settled 30,000 years ago by the migration of people from other area islands. Europeans landed on the island in 1568. In 1893, the British declared a protectorate over the Solomon Islands, making it a part of the British colonial empire. On 7 December 1941, the Japanese Empire attacked the American fleet on Pearl Harbor and other American, British and Dutch possessions throughout Southeast Asia and the Pacific. On 22 January 1942, the war came to the Solomon Islands when a Japanese plane dropped bombs on Gavutu Island. After that,

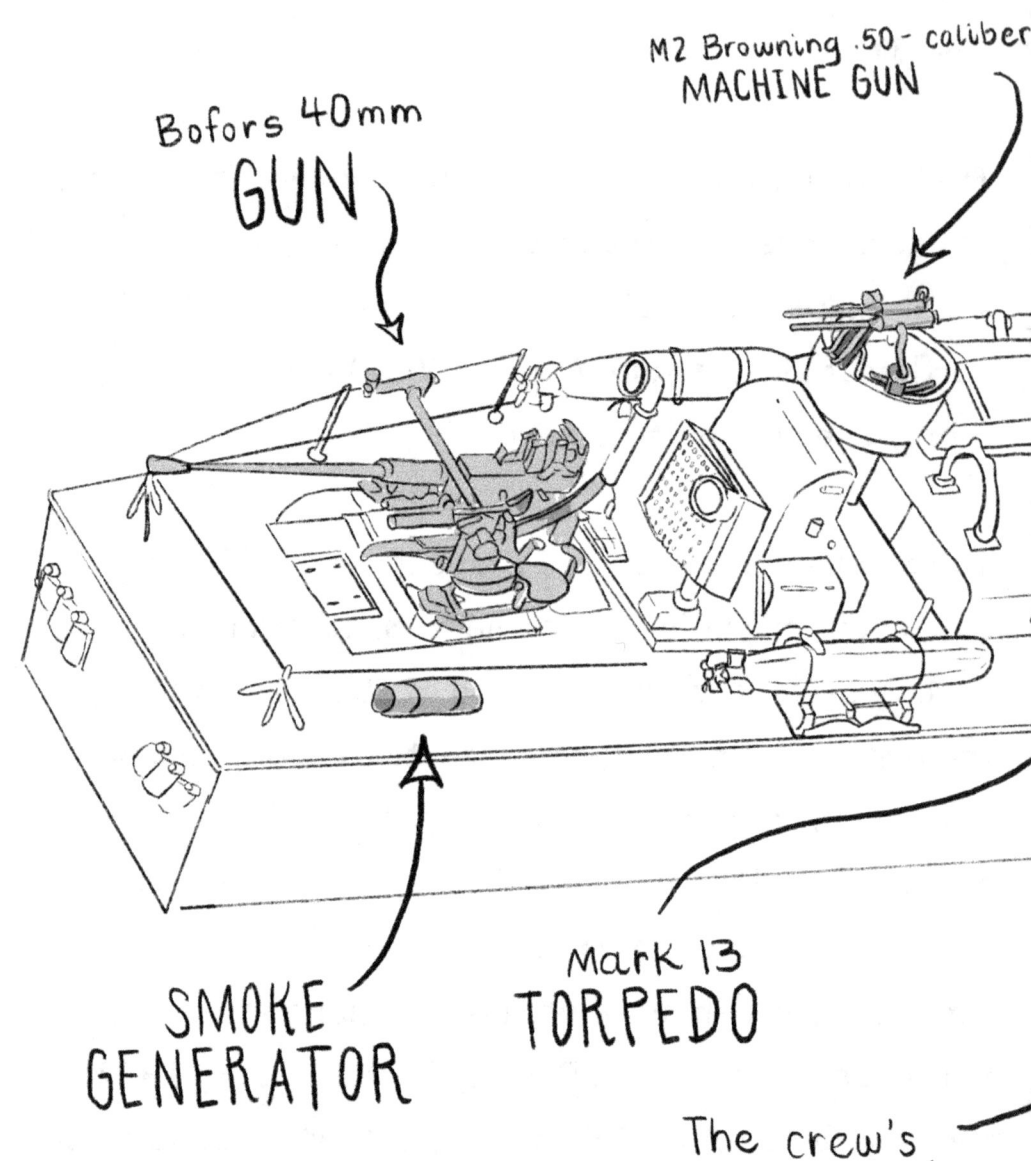

most Europeans evacuated to Australia. However, many who remained joined an operational network, the Coastwatchers, which had been established pre-war by the Royal Australian Navy (RAN) and was tasked with carrying out intelligence gathering in their various locations.

A turning point in the conflict came on 7 August 1942, when 11,000 United States soldiers landed on Guadalcanal and Tulagi. This began a campaign on the Solomon Islands that lasted for over a year, resulting in the deaths of 23,800 Japanese and 1,600 United States soldiers.

In support of this and other military campaigns, the Coastwatchers and their Scouts lived behind enemy lines. They observed and reported on Imperial Japanese military activities, enabling Allied forces to undertake attacks and battles with increasing confidence. The importance of this group was recognized by the Allied Commander of the South West

Pacific Area, Admiral 'Bull' Halsey USN, in 1944 when he said that "The Coastwatchers saved Guadalcanal, and Guadalcanal saved the Pacific."

One of the roles of the Coastwatchers was to rescue U.S. pilots downed in aerial fighting, as well as sailors whose vessels had sunk. Those rescued were passed back through the islands to their original base, where they could rejoin their units. One of the most acclaimed rescues was of Lieut. John Fitzgerald Kennedy and his crew of the patrol boat PT-109. For Solomon Islanders, these campaigns marked a new era in their history. This history continues to influence the social, political, and economic landscapes in the country today. Our hope that this book will inform young people of the heroism and courage of their forebearers.

For more information and
educational resources,
go to **www.alanelliott.com/PT109**

or scan the QR code

Anna "Annie" Kwai is a Solomon Islander from Malaita, a large mountainous island north of Guadalcanal. She is the author of the book Solomon Islanders in World War II: An Indigenous Perspective. Annie holds a master's degree in History from the Australian National University (ANU). She is passionate about Pacific History and has lectured on history at universities in the Solomon Islands and Papua New Guinea. She is currently a doctoral candidate in History at the ANU, exploring Solomon Islands' indigenous history concerning its neighbors and the world.

Alan C. Elliott has had 20+ books published, primarily history & technology, including books published by The History Press, Arcadia Publishing, CRC, Thomas Nelson, Sage, M.E. Sharp, and John Wiley & Sons. He also has two children's books published by Morrow Junior Books and Pelican. Alan holds two master's degrees (Data Analytics and Marketing.) He taught middle school and university-level courses for over 30 years, most recently at Southern Methodist University. He is a member of SCBWI and the Authors Guild. His website is www.alanelliott.com

Evelyn Morgan - is an illustrator and currently is pursuing a Bachelor of Fine Arts at the University of Texas in Arlington. She loves working with people who are passionate about using storytelling to represent local cultures well. Rescuing JFK was a joy to illustrate as she worked alongside local representative, Annie Kwai, to ensure that the Solomon Islanders' rich history was both respected and celebrated.

www.ingramcontent.com/pod-product-compliance
Lightning Source LLC
Chambersburg PA
CBHW072102290426
44110CB00014B/1794